Warm up the Winter

©Mary Merryweather Travis 2008

Published by Mad Jock Publishers

Liverpool, UK

www.madjockpublishers.com

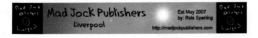

Mad Jock Publishers
Liverpool

Est May 2007
by: Rois Sperling
http://madjockpublishers.com

Dedication

~oOo~

That words can join hands, can become a communication of ideas, thoughts and emotions, is nothing less than a miracle, a gift to be shared and used, bringing together all who love to read, who live to write, or write to live. Words can brighten a frozen world, melt the hardest heart and bring tears to the most cynical of eyes.

I dedicate this book, this small collection of words, to my beautiful children whom I love more than life.

For Sam, strong harbour and true support through everything
For Chloe, beautiful, strong, brave daughter, confidante and friend
For Tom, my laughing place, my trusted partner in crime
For Bean, darling Bean, the fairy child who proves beyond doubt that angels exist
And for Pip, whose love and laughter warms my heart and lights up my world.

May God bless you, my darlings, for you are my hopes, dreams and my future. Walk tall and live strong.

Moo xx

Index

1. Softest silent night
(Shakespearean sonnet)
~oOo~

With quiet joy this Christmas Eve unfolds
in dancing glow of warming candle light
whilst tinsel gleams with shining greens and golds,
each adding to the beauty of this night.
A tree stands proudly dressed in festive cheer,
bright candy canes reach high to star of joy.
Sweet voices herald ending of a year
and tell the story of a baby boy.
A chair beside the crackling fire stands bare.
Before it, on the rug, a figure kneels
and gently bows a grateful head in prayer
of thanks for overwhelming love she feels.
A voice, which once was silent, rings out bright
with all the words of softest silent night.

~ooOoo~

2. A Human Mouse
(Elizabethan sonnet)

~oOo~

He hid, quite still upon the mantelshelf
'til all the festive fuss had come and gone.
"What is it for...." he pondered to himself,
"This decorated tree with candles on?
Why all these stockings, hung up by the fire,
so brightly hued and filled with papered glee?"
He scratched a whisker, pausing to admire
a tasty candy cane, hung on the tree.
A midnight hush fell over darkened room
just barely lit by coloured points of light.
A faint refrain rang softly through the gloom,
to sing to him of precious holy night.
And simple though the soul of mice must be,
he shed a gladdened tear, beneath that tree.

~ooOoo~

3. Tending the sheep
(Lilibonelle)

~oOo~

Soft, feathered snow lay deep upon the field
where gathered sheep awaited close of day,
whilst tranquil shepherd tended to their needs
with patient words and fragrant, sun cut hay.

~oOo~

Where gathered sheep awaited close of day,
gold dipped, each fleece, by sunset's lovely light,
the flaming evening rays outlined each bough
of snow brushed trees against the fall of night.

~oOo~

Whilst tranquil shepherd tended to their needs,
their grateful bleating soothed the wind's harsh howl
and left, within its stead, a peaceful song
which sang a close to evening's shadowed cowl.

~oOo~

With patient words and fragrant, sun cut hay,
the shepherd offered comfort to his flock
and marked, with each deep print upon the snow
a timeless pace which ticked to endless clock.

~oOo~

How beautiful, this glowing winter scene.
Could we, but keep a moment so serene.

~ooOoo~

4. Snow lover

(Rhyming couplets)

~oOo~

Running, top speed, panicked flight!
Fearing retribution, white!

~oOo~

Never should have done the dare,
mashed a snowball in his hair.

~oOo~

Quick, behind this tree I hide,
feel my wellies slip and slide.

~oOo~

Crash! I landed in a heap.
From tangled scarf and hat I peep...

~oOo~

Oh no! He's coming! Just can't move,
lost within my giggling groove.

~oOo~

Cold wet snowball down the neck!!
Soaking! Freezing! What the heck.

~oOo~

Pull him down with gales of laughter.
This, my happy ever after!

~ooOoo~

5. Beyond the rain
(Shakespearean sonnet)
~oOo~

Upon each life, of course the rain must fall.
Without it, how would roses bloom and grow
or seedlings sprout to oaken pillars tall,
if not for dreary rain or driving snow?
Within each life, young leaves must e'er grow old
and gentle blossoms fade to brown and die,
for would we forfeit Autumn's gown of gold
nor guard a seed, to plant when spring is nigh?
Into each life the sun will sometimes shine
and rainbows arch their promise in the sky.
In fleeting moments, wind and warmth combine
to dry those streams of tears we each must cry.
So light your winter coals when all seems bleak
and find, beyond the rain, the joy you seek.

6. Winter sunrise
(Optimus)
~oOo~

Close pressed, my face, on icy pane
as rose the sun in fiery blaze
and lighted every crystal chain
with diamond points in frosted maze.

A thousand tiny rainbows shine
And for one moment, each is mine!

~ooOoo~

7. Everlasting oak
(Quatrains)
~oOo~

She planted an acorn, the little girl,
and watered it from the stream,
enthralled as a tiny shoot unfurled
into promises, tender and green.

A promise of love, as the years passed by
where she lay, full entwined with another.
Then a beautiful promise of years yet to come
as the tree shaded baby and mother.

A grandmother rocks in a chair, by her tree.
Crabbed finger wears mourning ring.
She knowingly smiles as she pats the young oak
which, one day would shelter a king.

~ooOoo~

8. Winter river

(free verse)

~oOo~

Alive
with a million
iridescent spangles,
reflected sunlight dances
with all the joy of creation,
as the river calmly lays out its
azure beauty before my dazzled eyes.

Impervious
to the magnificence
of its moorings,
a tiny boat
bobs
impudently
amidst this
shimmering light show.

I smile softly,
amused by its irreverence.

If familiarity breeds contempt,
may I never see such beauty again
lest I fail to appreciate it.

~ooOoo~

9. You

(Free verse)
A guest poem by Bean
~oOo~

Without you, I am lost
forever in the midst of time
Without you next to me, I fear the dark.
Without you, I am cold.
Stay with me.

© Bean Travis 2007

~ooOoo~

10. Evening by the fire
(Whitney)
~oOo~

Winter nights
can get so cold!
Light a fire
and let's get warm.
Snuggled up
beneath fur throw.
You can warm your hands on me.

By the fire,
beneath fur throw,
hands get warm,
so does my nose.
Let me have
a hand or two,
I'll return that warmth to you

~ooOoo~

11. If not for you
(Double ethere)

~oOo~

Would
I have
known these joys,
if not for you?
A walk in the rain,
a simple supper, shared?
The blaze of an open fire
warms the flow of conversation.
Two mugs of cocoa steam on the hearth,
their rich aroma inviting and sweet.
You read to me the words of poets past.
Could I have enjoyed such a moment,
without the joy of your presence?
With memories still to make
and so much love to share,
I live each moment.
If not for you,
then I would
have known
none.

~ooOoo~

12. Clock
(Quatern)

~oOo~

Whilst the clock kept in perfect time,
with its deep and sonorous chime,
and the shadow grew longer still,
from the ancient spire, on the hill,

~oOo~

we started our long, downhill climb,
whilst the clock kept in perfect time.
The sound of the eventide song
rang sweet, as we hurried along.

~oOo~

The sun bid a charming good night.
We slowed, to the beautiful sight,
whilst the clock kept in perfect time
to the sound of Night's velvet rhyme.

~oOo~

Then home, to the warmth of the hearth,
a room filled with comfort and mirth,
where love played its gentle sublime,
whilst the clock kept in perfect time.

~ooOoo~

13. Beggars can be choosers
(Rhyming couplets)
~oOo~

So what now? came the question in the air.
What is there left? I shrugged, with weak despair.

What left to feel, to think, what more to lose?
What part of mind or body without bruise?

I held my head and wished away such ills;
I cursed events which brought such bitter pills

and looked no further than inside of me
for all the pain that I could bear to see.
But.......
Today, the sun shone full upon the street
where I lay weeping at my window seat

and lit upon a beggar, cold and thin.
I flung my window wide and called him in.

No clothes had he but rags, and chilled bare feet,
blue white with cold, and not a scrap to eat.

But on his face, the calmness of a saint
that artists far and wide would long to paint.

I asked, as anyone would want to know
what caused this ragged fellow's saintly glow.

He answered, with a smile which took my breath,
that God had shown him life beyond our death.

His shining face proclaimed his words no lie,
that we are promised 'only death will die'.

I rose, and claimed that promise for my own,
saved by what a starving man had thrown.

14. Back to bed

(Rhyming quatrains)

~oOo~

I wipe the mist from frosted window pane
and peer into the early light of day.
How chill this flagstone floor against my toes
when winter holds a morning in her sway

~oOo~

I scratch a hole and press my sleep warmed nose
against the cold opaque of silvered frost
in hope of seeking out the sunrise warmth
but every ray is wreathed in mist, and lost.

~oOo~

From kneeling vantage point on window seat,
I watch as sifting snowflakes dance and fly,
each one unique in crystal patterned host
of feathered flakes which float from frozen sky.

~oOo~

Then fast my naked feet on icy stones
to seek once more the comfort of my bed
and find again that dent of dream filled warmth
where moments past, I left my sleepy head.

~oooo

15. A fisherman's brew
(Elizabethan sonnet)
~oOo~

On bobbing boat in freezing winter sea
he rubs his hands and breathes a warming blow
on fingers stiff and gnarled, bereft of gloves
to offer them a woollen knitted glow.
The sky holds not one drop of sunlit heat
although its vast and cloud free depths are clear,
as if the heavens were a frozen land
reflecting back an icy blue veneer.
The whistle on the old tin kettle blows
announcing comfort's flow from steaming pot
and in appreciation of his tea,
the heavens frozen beauty is forgot.
As hands clasp steaming cup with heated glee,
he smiles, with gentle triumph, at the sea.

~ooOoo~

16. Unsung hero
(Shakespearean sonnet)
~oOo~

A darkened winter morning dawns too soon
to drag our weary hero from his rest.
The frosted sunrise hosts a pallid moon
which puts his sleep-filled courage to the test.
Blue denim armour, damp from heatless night,
its chills unwelcome to unready legs,
and sweater, knitted lovingly, but tight,
do little to dispel sleep's shivered dregs.
Descending creaking stairs with breath's abate,
so not to wake the babes ahead of time,
he drags his stiffened burden through the gate,
ignoring noxious stench and rotting slime.
The overflowing dustbins safe in place,
he heads indoors to start the breakfast race.

~ooOoo~

17. Rescued

(Rhyming quatrains)

~oOo~

I can almost feel the comfort of the firelight
as it flickers at the window, warm and red
and the cold outside cuts deep, but not as cruelly
as the longing for a hand upon my head.

~oOo~

I remember days long gone when there was laughter,
when the sound of children's voices filled my ears,
and caresses felt like happy ever after.
Now I sit alone, devoid of even tears.

~oOo~

As this choke cuts cruel and tight around my sorrow
and the water freezes, filthy in my bowl,
so I close my weary eyes upon tomorrow
which holds no hope nor joy for this sad soul.

~oOo~

Then a voice rings out with clear and present purpose
and hands release my throat from metal chain.
The faintest light of hope cuts through the darkness.
Could there be love and comfort, once again?

~oOo~

As you stroke my head, your hands speak of your sadness
and the tears you shed help wash my pain away .
My heart beats strong with new awakened gladness
as I walk with trust, towards a brighter day.

~oOo~

Now I lay my well fed warmth upon a hearthrug
whilst a gentle child sits reading by my side,
But for you, I'd still be chained and cruelly treated.
But for you, I would have lain in filth and died.

~ooOoo~

18. Summer Christmas
(Rhyming quatrains)

~oOo~

She asked him if he'd love her
for ever and a day.
He said he'd always loved her
and promised that he'd stay.

~oOo~

"When Christmas comes in August"
he always used to say,
"Until the time that happens,
I'll never go away!"

~oOo~

She'd laugh and hold him tightly,
a game they'd often play,
and tell him that she'd love him
for ever and a day.

~oOo~

The years rolled mellow forward
as both grew old and grey.
He never failed to cherish,
she'd honour and obey.

~oOo~

Then, on a golden summer,
there came a price to pay
as he fell sick and left her
although he'd tried to stay.

~oOo~

She wept as she remembered,
that game they used to play.
How could he break his promise
and leave her in this way?

~oOo~

But, as she sat in sorrow
that sunny August day,
a snowflake gently kissed her
to the tune of far off sleigh.

~ooOo~

19. Imagine this?
(Rhyming couplets)
~oOo~

Imagine a world where a camel could tell you the time!
Or a pig with a penchant for fruity, Italian wine.

~oOo~

Can you picture a rainstorm where only the flowers got wet?
Or a magical sun which would sing you to sleep as it set?

~oOo~

Think of thunder which plays with the charm and finesse of a band
And beaches where mermaids and little girls played in the sand.

~oOo~

If "too good to be true!" turned out better than ever it seemed,
And a clever machine could allow you to choose all your dreams!

~oOo~

Just imagine a world where the birdsong could stop all the strife
Or a home where I'd see you at least every day of my life.

20. Never mind the roses
(Free style)
~oOo~

How happy, to love when the sun shines bright,
when the world seems to spin to your tune,
to chance a romance on warm summer night
by the light of a silvery moon.
How carefree and easy the laughter we share
at a tide that keeps turning our way,
to shake off the raindrops which land in the hair
if that's all that dampens the day.
But strength that you find in the troubles which rise
is more lasting than fair weather fun.
If the one by your side dries the tears in your eyes
when the day and the dancing are done,
then no matter what mountains to climb, nor what storm
should beset you when summer is gone
you have found solid gold in the hand that you hold,
and you know that such love will fight on.

~ooOoo~

21. It's not so bad!
(Free style)
~oOo~

Children grow up!
Well they'd have to grow up
or else they'd die young
and that's not what we want them to do!
So just do your best,
let the world do the rest
and give all the credit to you!

People grow old!
Of course they grow old!
Forever's not young
and that's how long we'd like to live on.
But your memories stay
at the end of the day
of all that you've been and have done.

Time flies so fast!
Well, the world won't stand still
and no wishing it will
could turn Father Time on his head!
So laugh life away,
welcome each fleeting day.
Time will stop soon enough when we're dead.

~ooOoo~

22. Winter web
(free style)

~oOo~

In hushed and silvered strands
of intricate align,
hung soft with morning's gems
that catch the sun and shine,
the web which binds the space
and sparkles with each dance
of Winter's frosted face
seems but a dream built chance
yet holds within each thread
more strength than hawsered rope.
Caught fast within its spread
are countless gleams of hope.

~oooo~

23. A place of her own
(Rhyming quatrains)
~oOo~

The house stood neglected and empty,
as she viewed with a critical eye.
There was space for a cot in the bedroom
and the colours were soft to the eye.
~oOo~
The sitting room windows were massive
with the sun beaming through at midday,
and the very old kitchen was charming
in a truly historical way.
~oOo~
The range in the hearth place was gleaming
with a liberal coat of black lead
inviting her into its aura
of wood smoke and freshly baked bread.
~oOo~
A thoughtful walk into the garden
confirmed all she'd thought she would find.
There were fountains, and benches to sit on;
a much needed place to unwind.
~oOo~
The dining hall housed a huge fireplace
with the ashes of yesteryear's fire.
It spoke of an old pace of living
which she'd rapidly come to desire.
~oOo~

All the modern formalities covered,
the contracts were signed in a week.
She moved on a wet, windy Sunday,
relieved that the roof didn't leak.

~oOo~

Much arranging and more re-arranging
'til the furniture looked quite at home.
Her armchair sat right by the fireplace
and they'd even connected the phone.

~oOo~

As she settled herself for the evening
with the heat from the fire on her face,
a calm and content fell upon her
as she sank, with a sigh, into place.

~oOo~

The winter wind whipped down the chimney;
it whistled and sang in the flame
and in it she heard her acceptance,
as the grateful house whispered her name.

~ooOoo~

24. Long forgotten Sunday
(Elizabethan sonnet)

~oOo~

Insubstantial wisps of fingered mist,
whose slender beckon could not be denied,
enticed me into ancient shaded tryst
where all I held as fact fell hushed and died.
Above me rang a long forsaken chime
to call the disremembered to their prayer,
whilst organ notes from hymns of bygone time
fell rich from pipes and keys no longer there.
Pellucid in their olden Sunday best
a congregation sat in reverent praise
Lace bonnets, waistcoats, children quaintly dressed,
each met my glance with kind, accepting gaze.
And as their voices rose in gentle psalm
I found, within myself, a long lost calm.

25. Let the wind blow
(Petrachan sonnet)

Warm firelight draws us into its surround
and autumn whisks the leaves from helpless trees
to scatter them with wild and wind torn breeze
upon the russet blanket of the ground,
as sleepy children nest in my embrace
all bathed and combed, and wrapped in cosy gowns
for bedtime tales of teddy bears and clowns
which bring a spellbound smile to every face.
When winter knocks with eager frosted hand
and rattles at the panes with icy blast,
whilst yet another season breathes its last
in picturesque and snowfall covered land,
I give you hope of laughter yet to share
in creaking comfort of this fireside chair.

26. Welcome Inn
(Rhyming quatrains)
~oOo~

Unlatch the heavy, studded, oaken door,
but just a crack, to keep the warmth within
and draw the woven curtain back before
you peer into the heart of Welcome Inn.

~oOo~

Around the ancient bar, on perching stools
a group of lively youngsters spread some cheer
with jokes of ribald humour learned at schools
but best enjoyed with comradeship and beer.

~oOo~

The lusty, busty barmaid smiles her thanks
for tip tucked into ringed and work worn hand,
whilst laughing at the eager schoolboys pranks
drowned out in part by local farmer band.

~oOo~

Old Si attacks the violin with force
competing with his cousin on the drums
and though their voices may be rough and coarse,
enthusiasm shines from toothless gums!

~oOo~

And in the armchairs by the roaring fire
with tapping toes and wine warmed tranquil smiles
the walking stick brigade surround the squire,
who owns the land around the inn for miles.

~oOo~

The fireplace leaks a gust of woodscent smoke
inducing some complaint with hearty cough
and cries of "Landlord! Chimney needs a poke,
before it sets the Major's asthma off!"

~oOo~

From back behind the bar, 'mine host' appears
and lifts the shotgun down with scant ado,
then shouting to them all to block their ears,
he fires both barrels off to clear the flue!

~oOo~

Job done, he takes a bow to loud applause
and firmly shakes a local hand or two,
whilst on the roof an outraged raven caws,
forsaking peril's perch for pastures new!

~oOo~

The smoke has cleared; fresh logs spit sparks with verve,
as band refresh their voices 'on the house'
with ice cold cider, kept in cool reserve
and served with smiles by landlord's cheerful spouse.

~oOo~

Push wide the door, as all eyes turn and stare
and landlord bids you warmly "Come on in"
You'll find a rare, unrivalled aura there
amongst the folk who fill the Welcome Inn.

27. A breath of fresh air.
(Shakespearean sonnet)
~oOo~

Such playful breeze of salted, sea-blown air,
advantaged by my sun-warmed soft mien,
mischievous, snatched the ribbon from my hair
and blew it far beyond my reach or ken.
Fast frenzied whipped those curls of silken calm
upon the impish whim of smiling wind,
beyond a hope of smooth recovered charm
nor that which shell-filled hands could yet rescind.
With laughter at such instant disarray,
reluctant still to drop my treasured find,
I sat on sand by ocean's sparkled spray
and let that sea breeze play where it had mind.
I wish you could have seen how good it felt,
to blow away such cares as life had dealt.

28. Umbrella
(Free style)
~oOo~

Hushed whisper of the sleeping autumn leaves
soft crushed where gentle lovers lie, entwined
as waning sun through naked branches weaves
its hopes of shadowed promises to find.
And crisp, the freshened wind brings colder storm
with icy touch, forerunning winter's chill,
but blanketed by words which soothe and warm
within such lines as strengthen mind and will,
two souls take shelter in each other's thoughts
that pain and darkened days should count for naught.

~ooOoo~

29. Parallel winter
(Elizabethan sonnet)

~oOo~

Although these muddied boots progress alone
across the bridge where time has frozen still,
where autumn leaves lie piled where they have blown
and swirling forest brook runs fast downhill,
yet still I see the prints where you have walked
and feel your presence linger where I stand,
as if we had, at one time, stood and talked
or wandered here together, hand in hand.
The trees stretch out their arch of leafless boughs,
a sparse cathedral roof beneath the sky
and whisper with what voice the wind allows
that we shall sing together, by and by.
This path is narrow, as you say, and old,
but lined by mellow rock of promised gold

~ooOoo~

30. Silver Lake
(Free verse)

For Dawn

Moon on the winter lake
lends a peaceful
lavender hue
to the night.

Spirit passes lightly,
beyond silvered,
frosted trees.

White gown gleams
with luminescence,
owing nothing to
ice reflected moonlight.

Drifting serene forever,
in beauteous tranquillity,
she casts no shadow on
the frozen lake

only a faint shimmer of gladness
that she was ever there.

~ooOoo~

31. Counting sheep and blessings
(Shakespearean sonnet)
~oOo~

These hours that pass should find me lost in sleep
but still this heartless clock marks out each chime,
and I, unwilling company to keep,
await with restless ire the march of time.
How silent and how slowly drifts this night,
with every minute stretching out its length,
abetted by the moon's attentive light
which stares me out with sleepless, silvered strength.
No whispered words of heavy lidded calm,
nor mesmeric companion's even breath.
Remembered feel of warm, encircled arm
brings harsh the true finality of death
and. with such thought, a wry and grateful smile
that I may pace this clock a further while.

~ooOoo~

32. Grandpa's garden
(Lilibonelle)

for Grandpa Travis

Narrow path of well trod ash and cinders,
edged with rough hewn boards of weathered wood
where tiny, sturdy boots with haste tied laces
on small plump legs in frock and muslin hood.

Edged with rough hewn boards of weathered wood,
the garden path led winding through the flowers,
where Grandpa bent his solemn knowing gaze
to reds and pinks for glorious tranquil hours.

Where tiny, sturdy boots with haste tied laces
stand patiently observing Grandpa's choice
of roses, phlox and daisies in a bouquet,
each flower named in Grandpa's gentle voice.

On small plump legs, in frock and muslin hood
with both hands clasped behind her satin sash,
the little girl makes memories of Grandpa,
along his garden path of cindered ash.

~ooOoo~

33. All the rivers ran
(Elizabethan sonnet)

~oOo~

I lay as in a dream on silver cloud
which softly sighed in simple solitude,
obscuring, with its incandescent shroud,
the tear-filled mists of sorrow's soft intrude.
A tender touch upon a waiting hand,
in gentle luminescent light surround
as drifts of thoughts began to understand
the nature of the spirit they had found.
Then rivers ran, to join with weeping seas
which lapped in timeless rhythm of despair
at lonely sands, abandoned by the breeze
of possibilities no longer there.
One single diamond drop of love welled free
to run down hills of hope towards your sea.

~oo○oo~

34. Sculptured
(Variant quatrains)
~oOo~

He stands amidst the seasoned green of nature
where edge of lawn submits to bordered bed.
Perfection in his timeless marble outlines
from high arched feet to noble, sculptured head.

With eyes which hold the wisdom of the sightless
he watches ages pass and ages dawn,
as frail old men play chess at morning tables,
in chairs which rusted long ere they were born.

The babes at play, whilst white capped matrons gossip,
look up with laughter at his marbled charms,
whilst tiny, dimpled girls make daisy bracelets
to wear with pride on tiny, dimpled arms.

Then tranquil afternoon brings welcomed colour
as boys in collared suits fly kites with tails
which stream, magnificent in brightest splendour,
upon each leaf strewn rush of autumn gales.

An evening graces skies with rosy beauty,
which fades to quiet velvet of the night,
and still he stands, with centuries enjoyment
of stars on constant path of dusted light,
and gazes quite serene, from sculptured height.

~ooOoo~

35. The Minstrel
(Sestina)

~oOo~

The road knew well the rhythm of his feet
as in the dust he travelled blithely on,
sharing at each settlement he passed
where faces gathered just to hear him play.
Calloused, work worn hands clapped out their joy
forgetting for a moment burden's weight.

~oOo~

As though his agile body bore no weight
he danced and sprang on jingle bell clad feet
which brought forth smiles of momentary joy
from little ones whose childhood had moved on
without a chance to caper, or to play
whilst sunny days in drudge and hardship passed.

~oOo~

An hour of merry music too soon passed,
returning them the toil but not the weight.
For in the sombre heads a song would play
and haunting rhythm lift those dragging feet.
And though the days of poverty drove on
a corner of each heart remembered joy.

~oOo~

So filled the minstrel's days with dance and joy
he scarce acknowledged how the years had passed
but with his lute and light heart, wandered on.
Nor did he take much heed of all the weight
that time exacted from those bell clad feet,
but lost his age in merriment and play.

~oOo~

Soon, all who gathered round to sing and play,
or glean from precious song and tales, some joy,
began to notice that his prancing feet
seemed heavier with every year which passed
and struggled now to bear his fragile weight,
but bravely danced the aging minstrel on.

~oOo~

The road now seemed to wind forever on.
What, years before had seemed but children's play
now felt an almost unfeasible weight;
the task of spreading music, tales and joy.
Too soon, the minstrel's dancing days had passed
and stillness now befell those nimble feet.

~oOo~

Now he looks on with gentle joy,
while others play the songs he passed,
and takes his weight from worn out feet.

~ooOoo~

36. Winter
(Free verse)

A guest poem by Pip aged 7

Winter as never before;
grey mists, never ending silence.
As I walk in soft snow
I feel a chilling breeze glow
throughout the forest.
Wolves howl.
A small hibernating animal
opens one sleepy eye
to stare as the last leaf falls,
then curls back up again.
Winter seems forever.

© Pip Travis 2008

~ooOoo~

37. White over gold
(Terzanelle)

~oOo~

The faded autumn drooped its russet head
of richest glowing shades of brown and gold.
The faded autumn drooped its russet head
to watch the silver sprinkled frost take hold
as winter spread soft wilderness instead
of richest glowing shades of brown and gold.
And all the world became a frozen bed
whilst autumn hid beneath the powdered throw.
As winter spread soft wilderness instead
with dizzy dancing flakes of feathered snow,
each whirled and whisked aloft by frigid draught
whilst autumn hid beneath the powdered throw.
The lake, hard glassed where rosy children laughed
as brightly knitted scarves blew in the breeze
each whirled and whisked aloft by frigid draught
of whistling winds which danced through leafless trees.
The faded autumn drooped its russet head
as brightly knitted scarves blew in the breeze.
The faded autumn drooped its russet head.

~oooo~

38. Clayton Express
(Free style)

A guest poem by Tom

The bedraggled man rocked in his seat
as the trees, and the buildings, passed by.
He could not see much for the evening was dark,
and his hair blocked the view from his eyes.
Looking over his shoulder, he asked of a stranger,
in a deep and gravelly tone:
"Excuse me my dear
but I'm at a loss here!
What time does this train arrive home?"

The young lady in question looked worried,
taking note of his beard full of grime.
She replied to him
with a nervous grin
"Your guess is as good as mine."

Ten minutes later, they both left the carriage,
going their separate ways, but the night after next
(on that very same train)
the young lady again
took a seat.

From somewhere behind her,
a voice boomed like thunder:
"Excuse me my dear,
now I don't smell of beer

and in my hair creatures don't thrive!
My beard is neat and my new suit, complete.
Would you tell me what time we arrive?"

The young lady she spoke quite softly,
no longer concerned or repulsed.
"My dearest man,
we arrive in Sands
in less than a half of the hour."

"Thank you." he said
"Would you mind if I beg,
to escort you right safe to your home?"
"Perhaps" said she "you would join me for tea
and some home made cake or a scone?"

He gladly accepted her offer.
They were married, the first chance God gave.
which just goes to show
how far you can go
with a haircut, a wash and a shave!

© Tom Roy Sharp 2007

~ooOoo~

39. Faith

Did ever you feel the cruel frost
of winter's harshest bite,
yet not believe that spring would come
nor summer, warm and bright?

Do you have faith that the sky is blue?
That the love of man and wife
can soothe the pain of this evil world
and bless it with new life?

Did you ever see the look of love
'twixt mother and newborn child?
Or hear a father guide and teach
with words of wisdom, mild?

Do we blame God for man's inept
and sometimes wicked ways?
We all do, friend, yet still He says;
until the end of days.

~ooOoo~

40. Rain over my soul
(Elizabethan sonnet)

~oOo~

Drops of cooling rain from leaden sky
fall soft upon my upturned, heated face
and imitate the tears I cannot cry
for sadness locked inside a hidden place.
And brave, I smile, as snatches of refrain
ring out to tease the rain clouds as they weep,
and dance in splashing steps through pools of rain
awakening reflections from their sleep.
Mischievous wind which drives each scuttled cloud,
plays whispers with each teasing breath of air
as if to brush away this solemn shroud
which holds my heart a captive to its care.
My soul will not be bowed beneath this pain,
but dance in silent joy upon the rain.

~ooOoo~

41. Stormwalker

(Quatrains)

~oOo~

So I walked, in the storm and the rain,
with the wind whipping hard at my face
while the weather reflected my pain,
in this lonely and desolate place.

~oOo~

Bolts of thunder crashed loud in my ears
and I raged in despairing reply
whilst the rain, unrelenting, wept tears
but not once in my fury, did I.

~oOo~

In the turbulent dance of the trees
as the gales lashed in savage attack,
I could find unexpected release
from the devils which danced on my back.

~oOo~

Blue white lightning exploded the sky
in ferocious and phosphorous ire,
and I shook both my fists to defy
every outburst of flash tempered fire.

~oOo~

But the hurricane's passionate cloud
seemed to spend all my temper and ill,
for as fierce as the tempest raged loud
so my thoughts became gentler, and still.

~oOo~

So I walked through the storm and the rain
with relief streaming soft on my face,
and I found I had conquered my pain
in this storm torn, magnificent place.

~ooOoo~

42. Pine Crag Spire
(Quatrains)

~oOo~

These twisted, winter silhouettes
like shadows on the edge of light,
contort their cold unearthly forms
to brush the fabric of the night

and reach for skies which blister cold
with frosted stars on frozen flight
in tapestry of staring eyes
that weep in tears of feathered white

upon that needled carpet spread,
where pines had cast their scented fall,
and softly lie as dreams of ice
in drifting floats, which blanket all.

~ooOoo~

43. Time and time again

(Hourglass)

~oOo~

The old bandstand gently decays
with a crumbling air of romance
The weather and wind have their ways
as time makes its heartless advance.
Are the waltzes of bygone days
a trick of the light on your glance,
as you dreamily cast your gaze,
through history's timeless expanse?
Where a lone violin still plays
to the tune of a once loved dance
an ethereal shadow sways
in a misted, musical trance.
In a misted, musical trance,
An ethereal shadow sways
to the tune of a once loved dance.
where a lone violin still plays,
through history's timeless expanse.
as you dreamily cast your gaze,
a trick of the light on your glance
are the waltzes of bygone days.
As time makes its heartless advance
the weather and wind have their ways
With a crumbling air of romance
the old bandstand gently decays.

~ooOoo~

44. Starlight Serenade
(Sonnquain)

(For Culpers, who created this beautiful style)

An icy chill pervades the misted night
where frosted trees
in starkest freeze
gleam skeletal beneath the moon's cold light,

their twisted, leafless fingers, bloodless white,
shift in the breeze
like pointed pleas
against the winter's harsh, relentless bite.

And midnight owl in avaricious might
takes all he sees
with vicious ease
as though each killing were his given right.

Where callous moonlight casts its dappled shade,
some creature cries
to heartless skies,
a melancholy starlight serenade.

~ooOoo~

45. Morning beads
(Free verse)

A guest poem by Sam

Along carpeted halls,
boasting portraits of young life's tender memory,
the black guard watches with fixed gaze.
Friend or foe?
Only she can tell from atop her red tower.
Open swings the door,
warm light fills our faces to dry away cold tears.
Enter the room where my lord resteth,
a smile of contentment and a look of peace
upon his noble brow.
Dreams of eternal love fill his weary face.
I shall not wake him.
I will see him tomorrow.

© Sam sharp 2007

~ooOoo~

46. Christmas gift
(Shakespearean sonnet)
~oOo~

In early dark of frosted winter nights,
as windows show their decorated face
and eyes are drawn to tiny coloured lights
which cheerfully adorn each willing space,
I sit and gaze with wonder at the sky,
as if it were the first time ever seen,
and watch as tiny snowflakes twirl and fly
to mantel over autumn's gold and green.
The stars seem brighter now than times before.
Anticipation's magic fills the air
as in this waiting heart, an open door
swings wide to welcome joy, now you are there.
Within the softened glow of candles' light
I sing with you our song of silent night

~ooOoo~

47. Eyes of the Blind
(Quatrains)

~oOo~

Who says that you can't feel colours?
Who says that you can't smell red?
Whatever your senses tell you,
is the colour in your head.

~oOo~

The velvety rich of purple,
the springy bounce of green.
My hands have felt more colours
than most eyes have ever seen.

~oOo~

You can touch the warm yellow of sunlight
and the shivery white of snow.
The infinite blue of the sky above;
you don't need to see to know.

~oOo~

Walk out in autumn and sniff the brown
of your boots, as you splash through the mire!
Smell passionate depth in a blood red rose,
or the crackling orange of fire.

~oOo~

The soft, sweet pink of the lips of a child
when he kisses my cheek with love,
or that silvery feeling of peace of mind
as I stroke the wing of a dove.

~oOo~

So reach out with more than your vision.
Let colour flood into your mind.
You can catch all the light from the rainbow
if you look with the eyes of the blind.

~ooOoo~

48. Silk against my cheek
(Ottova rima)
~oOo~

The gentle waking cry of newborn child
compels me from the comfort of my bed.
My soft bare feet abhor this floor, so coldly tiled,
but mother love commands their forward tread.
My empty arms and tender heart beguiled
by tiny waving limbs and down-soft head.
I feel, against my cheek, her skin of silk,
as tiny daughter seeks her breakfast milk.

~ooOoo~

49. First kiss
(Shakespearean sonnet)

~oOo~

The blackness of the darkest hour of night
gave not the smallest hint of silvered beam
nor did the shrouded stars reveal their light
to guide the sightless sleeper through his dream.
Invisible within the velvet void,
the swelling ocean's whispered lullaby
to sailors on a ship she gently buoyed,
who slept, soft faced, as night crept silent by.
Then, almost unimaginably faint,
by delicate and skilful strokes of brush,
a rosy streak of master artist's paint
across the eastern stretch of starless hush.
With wondrous shades of frosted ruby bliss
the winter dawn bequeathed us her first kiss.

~ooOo~

50. Lac Clair (lake of light)
(Quatrains)

For Clare Lake

Where Winter had played, with cold sweetness, a filigree tune,
the lake's gentle lapping had ceased as though time was delayed.
The stark, frozen surface reflected the lavender moon,
a vast silver mirror caught fast in a timeless, blue glade.

The trees, frosted statues, stood bathed in mysterious light;
an army of black silhouettes which stood guarding the lake,
each branch casting shadows that lengthened with passage of night
like dark reaching fingers of giants that slowly awake.

The cover of deep, soundless snowflakes but whispered its fall,
as it feathered the ground and the trees with a delicate trace
that softened the shape of the silence which blanketed all
and sparkled in crystal cut tears on the moon's frosted face.

Like a star that had fallen, to shine on the bank of the lake,
overhung by the sharp fringe of icicles edging the trees,
a snowdrop, courageous portent of the spring's promised break
pushed its tiny face up through the Winter to nod in the breeze.

The moonlight caressed with light fingers, one diamond spun tear
that shimmered and shone 'ere it fell to the white dusted ground.
As icicles wept in cascade from their frozen veneer,
the gentle approach of the Spring sung a comforting sound.

~ooOoo~

51. Warm up the winter

(Rhyming quatrains)

~oOo~

Oh bring on your winter and bring on your snow!
In bright hats and mittens, a-rambling we'll go.
With dog's eager questing and children aglow,
come bring on your winter! Come play in this snow!

~oOo~

Lie down in white softness, your senses beguiled
by artistic angels and snowmen with smiles.
The treetops, the roof tops wear whiteness for miles!
Let's stack up our snowballs, white missiles in piles!

~oOo~

Oh bring on your snow fights and drag out your sled!
Cut armfuls of holly with berries of red.
There's time to complain of the cold when you're dead!
We'll warm up the winter with laughter instead.

~ooOoo~